Women Of
Modern Music

Project Manager: Carol Cuellar
Editorial Consultant: Larry Kornblum
Cover Design: Joseph Klucar

Title	Artist	Page

FOOLISH GAMES

Words and Music by
JEWEL KILCHER

Moderately slow ♩ = 66

(with pedal)

Verse:

1. You took_____ your___ coat off_____ and stood in the

2.3.4. *See additional lyrics*

rain,_____ you're al-ways cra - zy like_ that._____

And I watched_ from my___ win - dow, al-ways felt I was

* *Vocal sung one octave lower*

Foolish Games - 3 - 1

4

Verse 2:
You're always the mysterious one with
Dark eyes and careless hair,
You were fashionably sensitive
But too cool to care.
You stood in my doorway with nothing to say
Besides some comment on the weather.
(To Pre-Chorus:)

Verse 3:
You're always brilliant in the morning,
Smoking your cigarettes and talking over coffee.
Your philosophies on art, Baroque moved you.
You loved Mozart and you'd speak of your loved ones
As I clumsily strummed my guitar.

Verse 4:
You'd teach me of honest things,
Things that were daring, things that were clean.
Things that knew what an honest dollar did mean.
I hid my soiled hands behind my back.
Somewhere along the line, I must have gone
Off track with you.

Pre-Chorus 2:
Excuse me, think I've mistaken you for somebody else,
Somebody who gave a damn, somebody more like myself.
(To Chorus:)

From "MY BEST FRIEND'S WEDDING"

I SAY A LITTLE PRAYER

Words by
HAL DAVID

Music by
BURT BACHARACH

From the Touchstone Motion Picture "CON AIR"

HOW DO I LIVE

Words and Music by
DIANE WARREN

How Do I Live - 4 - 1

How Do I Live - 4 - 2

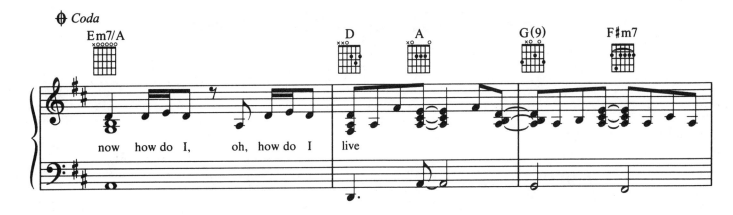

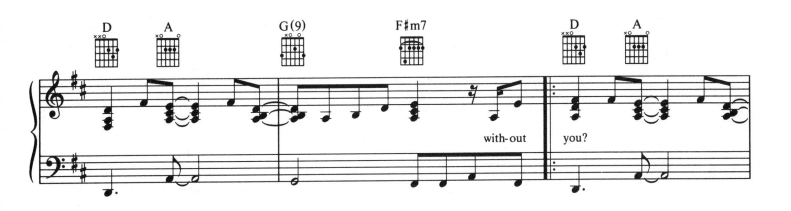

Repeat ad lib. and fade
(vocal 1st time only)

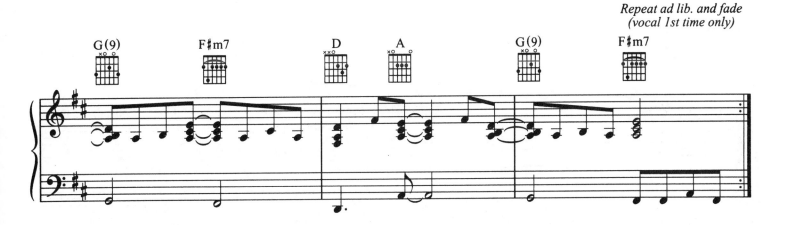

Verse 2:
Without you, there'd be no sun in my sky,
There would be no love in my life,
There'd be no world left for me.
And I, baby, I don't know what I would do,
I'd be lost if I lost you.
If you ever leave,
Baby, you would take away everything real in my life.
And tell me now...
(To Chorus:)

SAY YOU'LL BE THERE

Words and Music by
SPICE GIRLS and
ELIOT KENNEDY

Oh say you'll be there
I'm giv-ing you eve-ry-thing— all that joy—

—— can bring— this I swear.———   1. Last time

Say You'll Be There - 5 - 1

that we had__ this con-ver-sa-tion I de-ci-ded we should be friends,_____ yeah.

But now we're go-ing round__ in cir-cles tell me will this dé-jà vu nev-er end.__

Oh now you tell me that you've fall-en in love__ well I nev-
(Verses 2 & 3 see block lyric)

-er ev-er thought that would be,_____ yeah. This time you

18

Say You'll Be There - 5 - 3

Verse 2:

If you put two and two together you will see what our friendship is for,
If you can't work this equation then I guess I'll have to show you the door,
There is no need to say you love me it would be better left unsaid.

I'm giving you everything all that joy can bring this I swear,
And all that I want from you is a promise you will be there,
Yeah I want you.

Verse 3: (Instrumental)
Any fool can see they're falling, gotta make you understand.
To Coda

YOU WERE MEANT FOR ME

Words and Music by
JEWEL KILCHER and STEVE POLTZ

You Were Meant for Me - 5 - 1

Verse 2:
I called my mama, she was out for a walk.
Consoled a cup of coffee, but it didn't wanna talk.
So I picked up a paper, it was more bad news,
More hearts being broken or people being used.
Put on my coat in the pouring rain.
I saw a movie, it just wasn't the same,
'Cause it was happy and I was sad,
And it made me miss you, oh, so bad.
(To Chorus:)

Verse 3:
I brush my teeth and put the cap back on,
I know you hate it when I leave the light on.
I pick a book up and then I turn the sheets down,
And then I take a breath and a good look around.
Put on my pj's and hop into bed.
I'm half alive but I feel mostly dead.
I try and tell myself it'll be all right,
I just shouldn't think anymore tonight.
(To Chorus:)

I DON'T WANT TO

Words and Music by
R. KELLY

Verse:

real - ly don't feel like talk - ing on the phone,_____ and I
real - ly don't feel like smil - ing an - y - more,_____ and I

real - ly don't feel like com - pa - ny_____ at home. Late - ly,
have - n't had the peace to sleep____ at all. Ev - er

I don't want to do the things I____ used to do, ba - by,
since you went a - way, ba - by, my whole___ life has changed, I don't

since_____ I lost_____ you._____ } And I don't
wan - na love and I don't wan - na live._____ } And I don't

I WANT TO COME OVER

Words and Music by
MELISSA ETHERIDGE

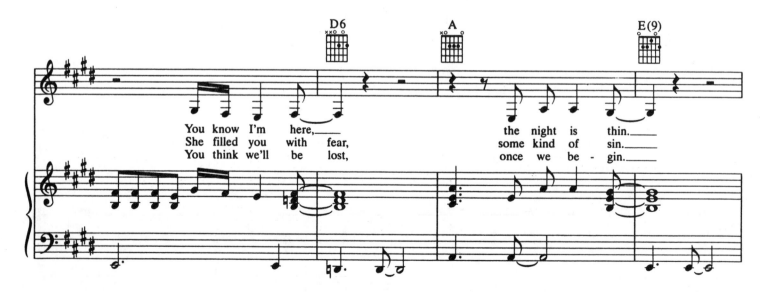

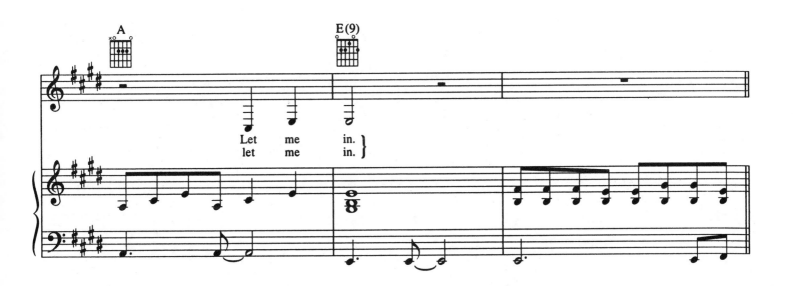

32

I Want to Come Over - 6 - 4

From the Motion Picture "THE PREACHER'S WIFE"

I BELIEVE IN YOU AND ME

Words and Music by
SANDY LINZER and DAVID WOLFERT

1. I be-lieve in you___ and me, I be-lieve that
2. *See additional lyrics*

we will be in love e-ter-nal-ly.___ Well, as far as I can see,

I Believe in You and Me - 4 - 1

38

2.
Bridge:
B
D♯m7
G♯m7
D♯m7
G♯m7
me.
May - be I'm a fool to feel the way I do.
mf
C♯m7
C♯m(maj7)
C♯m7
C♯m7/F♯
N.C.
Dm7/G
I would play the fool for - ev - er just to be with you for - ev - er.
3. I be - lieve in
Verse:
C
C/B♭
Fmaj9
mir - a - cles, and love's a mir - a - cle. And yes, ba - by, you're my dream come true.
Fm7/B♭
A♭/B♭
B♭/A♭
Fmaj7
C/G
Em7
Am7
I was lost, now I'm free, oh ba - by, 'cause

Verse 2:
I will never leave your side,
I will never hurt your pride.
When all the chips are down,
I will always be around,
Just to be right where you are, my love.
Oh, I love you, boy.
I will never leave you out,
I will always let you in
To places no one has ever been.
Deep inside, can't you see?
I believe in you and me.
(To Bridge:)

ALL I WANT

Words and Music by
IAN BROUDIE and PETER COYLE

All I Want - 5 - 1

42

All I Want - 5 - 3

Verse 2:
Confidence, coincidence,
Call it a sin, it's just like people say.
Tomorrow's here so open up your eyes,
Never hesitate.

Chorus 2:
All I want, all I wanna do
Is make you listen from now on.
Sleepin' in the dark, dreamin' of the stars,
Keep one to wish on from now on.

Chorus 3:
All I wanna do, all I wanna do,
You better listen from now on.
Open arms or cryin' eyes, say "Hello" or wave goodbye,
Which one are you thinking of ?

Because You Loved Me
(Theme from "Up Close & Personal")

Words and Music by
DIANE WARREN

Because You Loved Me - 5 - 1

BITCH

Words and Music by
SHELLY PEIKEN and MEREDITH BROOKS

Bitch - 5 - 1

54

way.___ I'm a bitch, I'm a tease, I'm a god-dess on my knees. When you

hurt, when you suf-fer, I'm your an-gel un-der-cov-er. I've been numb, I'm re-vived, you can't

say I'm not a-live. You know I would-n't want it an-y oth-er way._____

Ooh,___ ooh,___ ooh. Ooh,___ ooh,___ ooh.

Bitch - 5 - 5

FOR YOU I WILL

Words and Music by
DIANE WARREN

For You I Will - 5 - 1

A CHANGE WOULD DO YOU GOOD

Words and Music by
SHERYL CROW, BRIAN MacLEOD
and JEFF TROTT

A Change Would Do You Good - 4 - 1

COME TO MY WINDOW

Words and Music by
MELISSA ETHERIDGE

Verse 2:
Keeping my eyes open, I cannot afford to sleep.
Giving away promises I know that I can't keep.
Nothing fills the blackness that has seeped into my chest.
I need you in my blood, I am forsaking all the rest.
Just to reach you,
Just to reach you.
Oh, to reach you.
(To Chorus:)

COUNT ON ME

Words and Music by
BABYFACE, WHITNEY HOUSTON
and MICHAEL HOUSTON

Count on Me - 6 - 1

Count on Me - 6 - 2

FALLING INTO YOU

Words and Music by
MARIE CLAIRE D'UBALDO,
BILLY STEINBERG and RICK NOWLES

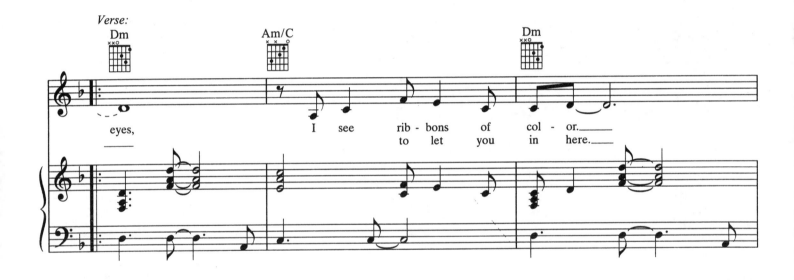

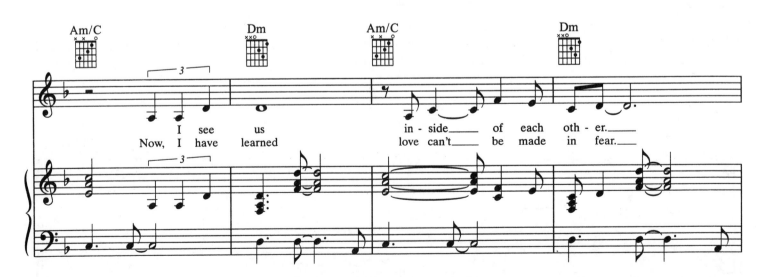

Falling into You - 5 - 1

From the Motion Picture "MICHAEL"

FEELS LIKE HOME

Words and Music by
RANDY NEWMAN

Feels Like Home - 5 - 1

Verse 2:
A window breaks down a long, dark street,
And a siren wails in the night.
But I'm alright 'cause I have you here with me,
And I can almost see through the dark, there's a light.
If you knew how much this moment means to me,
And how long I've waited for your touch.
If you knew how happy you are making me,
I've never thought I'd love anyone so much.
(To Chorus:)

FOUR LEAF CLOVER

Words and Music by
ABRA MOORE

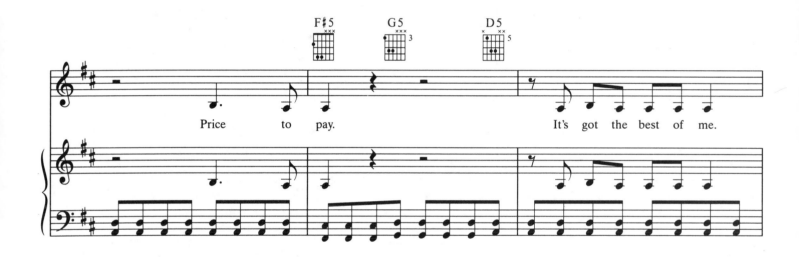

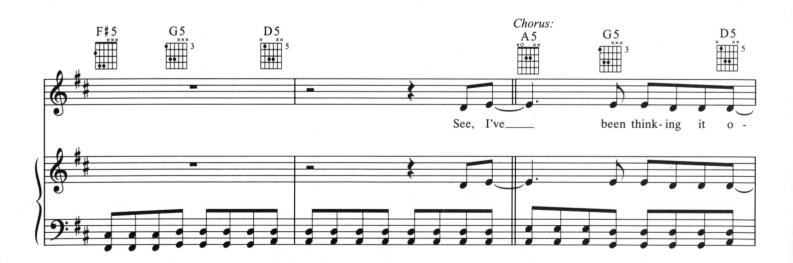

86

Four Leaf Clover - 6 - 3

I LOVE YOU ALWAYS FOREVER

Words and Music by
DONNA LEWIS

I Love You Always Forever - 5 - 1

"I Love You Always Forever" is inspired by the H.E. Bates novel *"Love for Lydia."*
Chorus/Bridge lyric courtesy of *Michael Joseph Ltd.* and *The Estate of H.E. Bates.*

Verse 3:
You've got the most unbelievable blue eyes I've ever seen.
You've got me almost melting away as we lay there
Under blue sky with pure white stars,
Exotic sweetness, a magical time.
(To Chorus:)

LET IT FLOW

Words and Music by
BABYFACE

*Vocal sung 1 octave lower.

Let It Flow - 5 - 3

From The Fox Searchlight Film, "THE BROTHERS McMULLEN"

I WILL REMEMBER YOU

Words and Music by
SARAH McLACHLAN, SEAMUS EGAN
and DAVE MERENDA

I Will Remember You - 4 - 1

Verse 2:
So afraid to love you,
More afraid to lose.
I'm clinging to a past
That doesn't let me choose.
Where once there was a darkness,
A deep and endless night,
You gave me everything you had,
Oh, you gave me life.
(To Chorus:)

(Optional Verse 1 — Album version)
Remember the good times that we had,
I let them slip away from us when things got bad.
Now clearly I first saw you smiling in the sun.
I wanna feel your warmth upon me,
I wanna be the one.
(To Chorus:)

KISSING YOU
(Love Theme From "ROMEO + JULIET")

Words and Music by
DES'REE and TIM ATACK

Kissing You - 4 - 1

Chorus:

ev - er. _____ 'Cause I'm _____ kiss- ing you, _____ oh. ___

I'm _____ kiss- ing you. ___

ONE OF US

Words and Music by
ERIC BAZILIAN

One of Us - 5 - 1

2 BECOME 1

Words and Music by
SPICE GIRLS, MATTHEW ROWEBOTTOM
and RICHARD STANNARD

2 Become 1 - 5 - 1

116

2 Become 1 - 5 - 4

Verse 2:

Silly games that you were playing, empty words we both were saying,
Let's work it out boy, let's work it out boy.
Any deal that we endeavour, boys and girls feel good together,
Take it or leave it, take it or leave it.
Are you as good as I remember baby, get it on, get it on,
'Cause tonight is the night when two become one.

I need some love like I never needed love before, (wanna make love to ya baby.)
I had a little love, now I'm back for more, (wanna make love to ya baby.)
Set your spirit free, it's the only way to be.

SUNNY CAME HOME

Words and Music by
SHAWN COLVIN and JOHN LEVENTHAL

Verse 1:

1. Sun-ny came home to her fa-v'rite room.___ Sun-ny sat down in the

Sunny Came Home - 6 - 1

WHAT ABOUT US
(From "Soul Food")

Moderately slow ♩ = 84

Words and Music by
MISSY ELLIOTT and TIM MOSLEY

1. Ba-by, I've seen you with an-oth-er
2. *See additional lyrics*

What About Us - 5 - 1

128

Verse 2:
Baby, I know that you've been pimpin'
Mr. Baller, trickin'.
Why'd you have to go, go and leave me?
Baby, I've always been your baby.
Love make a girl go crazy.
I can't understand why you left me.
(To Chorus:)

WHO WILL SAVE YOUR SOUL

Words and Music by
JEWEL KILCHER

Moderate shuffle feel ♩ = 112

Verse:

1. Peo - ple liv - in' their lives for you__ on T__ V,__ they say they're bet - ter than you__ and

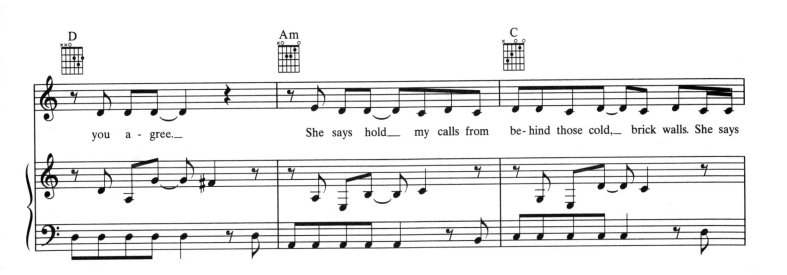

you a - gree.__ She says hold__ my calls from be - hind those cold,__ brick walls. She says

Who Will Save Your Soul - 7 - 1

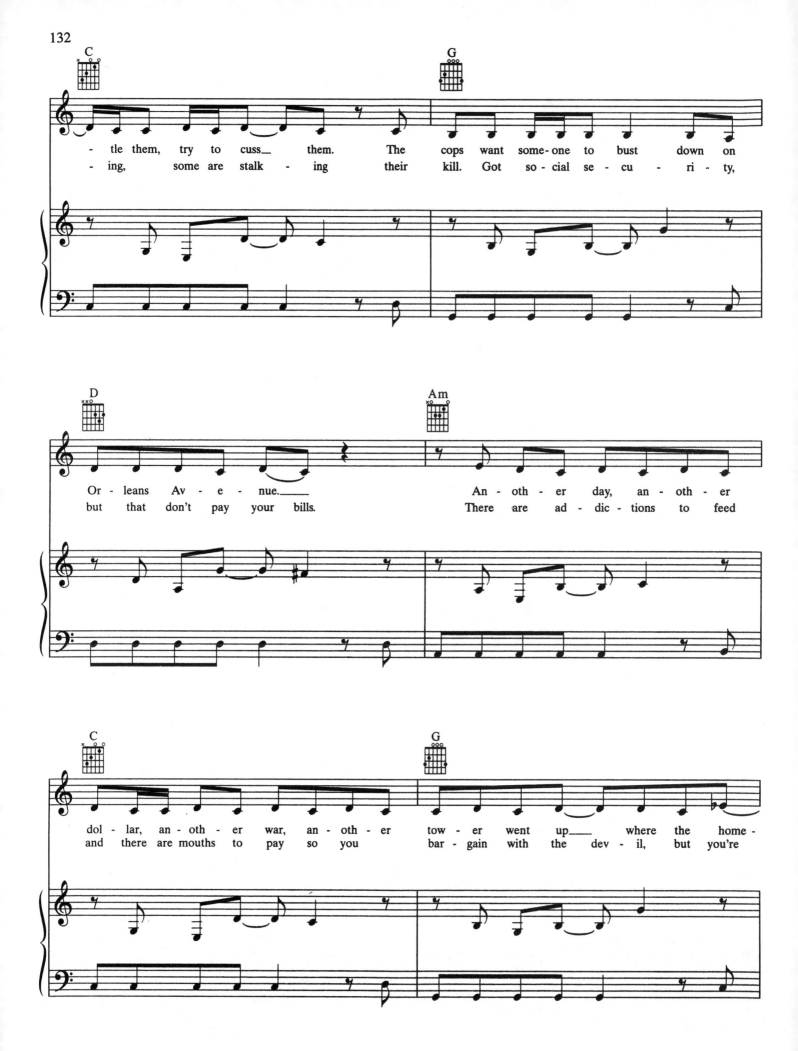

Who Will Save Your Soul - 7 - 5

134

YOU AND THE MONA LISA

Words and Music by
SHAWN COLVIN and
JOHN LEVENTHAL

1. Hold me down to an - y - thing,___ an - y - thing that you see.___
2. *See additional lyrics*

You and the Mona Lisa - 5 - 1

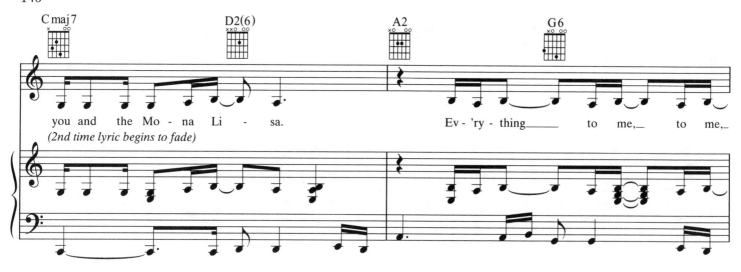

you and the Mo - na Li - sa.
(2nd time lyric begins to fade)

Ev - 'ry - thing_____ to me,__ to me,__

_____ to me,_____ to me.

Verse 2:
Nothing in particular and everything in between,
This is what you mean to me.
Only you and only me, climbing in the right direction,
On the way to everything.

Chorus 2:
We were walking up high,
And no one thought to try.
But I was the one to blame,
and it was just a mirage.
So I hid in the garage
'Til somebody called your name.
(Guitar Solo:)

YOU LIGHT UP MY LIFE

Words and Music by
JOE BROOKS

You Light Up My Life - 3 - 1

142

You Light Up My Life - 3 - 2

EVERYDAY IS A WINDING ROAD

Words and Music by
SHERYL CROW, BRIAN MacLEOD
and JEFF TROTT

*Tune guitar down 1/2 step

Everyday Is a Winding Road - 6 - 1

Verse:

3. I've been swim-ming in a sea of an - ar - chy.____ I've been liv-ing on

cof-fee and ni-co-tine. I've been won-d'ring if all____ the things I've_ seen were

WANNABE

Words and Music by
SPICE GIRLS, MATTHEW ROWEBOTTOM
and RICHARD STANNARD

Wannabe - 6 - 1

151

Wannabe - 6 - 2

154

If you wan-na be my lov-er.

Verse 2:
What do you think about that?
Now you know how I feel.
Say you can handle my love,
Are you for real?
I won't be hasty,
I'll give you a try.
If you really bug me,
Then I'll say goodbye.
(To Bridge:)

The Book of *Golden* Series

THE BOOK OF GOLDEN ALL-TIME FAVORITES
(F2939SMX) Piano/Vocal/Chords

THE BOOK OF GOLDEN BIG BAND FAVORITES
(F3172SMX) Piano/Vocal/Chords

THE BOOK OF GOLDEN BROADWAY
(F2986SMX) Piano/Vocal/Chords

THE NEW BOOK OF GOLDEN CHRISTMAS
(F2478SMB) Piano/Vocal/Chords
(F2478EOX) Easy Organ
(F2478COX) Chord Organ

THE BOOK OF GOLDEN COUNTRY MUSIC
(F2926SMA) Piano/Vocal/Chords

THE BOOK OF GOLDEN HAWAIIAN SONGS
(F3113SMX) Piano/Vocal/Chords

THE BOOK OF GOLDEN IRISH SONGS
(F3212SMX) Piano/Vocal/Chords

THE BOOK OF GOLDEN ITALIAN SONGS
(F2907SMX) Piano/Vocal/Chords

THE BOOK OF GOLDEN JAZZ
(F3012SMX) Piano/Vocal/Chords

THE NEW BOOK OF GOLDEN LATIN SONGS
(F3049SMX) Piano/Vocal/Chords

THE NEW BOOK OF GOLDEN LOVE SONGS
(F2415SOX) Organ

THE BOOK OF GOLDEN MOTOWN SONGS
(F3144SMX) Piano/Vocal/Chords

THE NEW BOOK OF GOLDEN MOVIE THEMES, Volume 1
(F2810SMX) Piano/Vocal/Chords

THE NEW BOOK OF GOLDEN MOVIE THEMES, Volume 2
(F2811SMX) Piano/Vocal/Chords

THE BOOK OF GOLDEN POPULAR FAVORITES
(F2233SMX) Piano/Vocal/Chords

THE BOOK OF GOLDEN POPULAR PIANO SOLOS
(F3193P9X) Intermediate/
Advanced Piano

THE BOOK OF GOLDEN ROCK 'N' ROLL
(F2830SMB) Piano/Vocal/Chords

THE NEW BOOK OF GOLDEN WEDDING SONGS
(F2265SMA) Piano/Vocal/Chords